RIPRAP

and

COLD MOUNTAIN POEMS

by

GARY SNYDER

North Point Press
Farrar, Straus and Giroux
New York

LIBRARY OF CONGRESS
CATALOGING-IN-PUBLICATION DATA
Snyder, Gary.
  [Riprap]
  Riprap; and, Cold Mountain poems/by
  Gary Snyder.
     p.   cm.
  I. Snyder, Gary. Cold Mountain
  poems.   1990.
  II. Title.   III. Title: Riprap.   IV. Title:
  Cold Mountain poems.
[PS3569.N88R5   1990]
811'.54—dc20   90-7639

Riprap was first published by the Origin
Press in 1959; "Cold Mountain Poems" were
first published in *Evergreen Review*, no. 6, in
1958. The two appeared together for the first
time in a volume published by the Four
Seasons Foundation in 1969.

This book is dedicated to:
SPEED MCINTURFF
ED MCCULLOUGH
BLACKIE BURNS
JIM BAXTER
ROY RAYMONDS
ROY MARCHBANKS
SPUD MURPHY
JACK PERSCHKE
JOE DUPERONT
JACK HAYWOOD
STANLEY PORTER
CRAZY HORSE MASON
In the woods & at sea.

CONTENTS

RIPRAP

*riprap: a cobble of stone laid on steep,
slick rock to make a trail for horses in
the mountains*

MID–AUGUST AT SOURDOUGH MOUNTAIN LOOKOUT

Down valley a smoke haze
Three days heat, after five days rain
Pitch glows on the fir-cones
Across rocks and meadows
Swarms of new flies.

I cannot remember things I once read
A few friends, but they are in cities.
Drinking cold snow-water from a tin cup
Looking down for miles
Through high still air.

THE LATE SNOW & LUMBER STRIKE
OF THE SUMMER OF FIFTY-FOUR

Whole towns shut down
    hitching the Coast road, only gypos
Running their beat trucks, no logs on
Gave me rides. Loggers all gone fishing
Chainsaws in a pool of cold oil
On back porches of ten thousand
Split-shake houses, quiet in summer rain.
Hitched north all of Washington
Crossing and re-crossing the passes
Blown like dust, no place to work.

Climbing the steep ridge below Shuksan
    clumps of pine
    float out the fog
No place to think or work
    drifting.

On Mt. Baker, alone
In a gully of blazing snow:
Cities down the long valleys west
Thinking of work, but here,
Burning in sun-glare
Below a wet cliff, above a frozen lake,
The whole Northwest on strike
Black burners cold,
The green-chain still,

I must turn and go back:
        caught on a snowpeak
        between heaven and earth
And stand in lines in Seattle.
Looking for work.

PRAISE FOR SICK WOMEN

1

The female is fertile, and discipline
(contra naturam) only
        confuses her
Who has, head held sideways
Arm out softly, touching,
A difficult dance to do, but not in mind.

Hand on sleeve: she holds leaf turning
            in sunlight on spiderweb;
Makes him flick like trout through shallows
Builds into ducks and cold marshes
Sucks out the quiet: bone rushes in
Behind the cool pupil a knot grows
Sudden roots sod him and solid him
Rain falls from skull-roof mouth is awash
            with small creeks
Hair grows, tongue tenses out—and she

Quick turn of the head: back glancing, one hand
Fingers smoothing the thigh, and he sees.

2

Apples will sour at your sight.
Blossoms fail the bough,
Soil turn bone-white: wet rice,
Dry rice, die on the hillslope.

All women are wounded
Who gather berries, dibble in mottled light,
Turn white roots from humus, crack nuts on stone
High upland with squinted eye
          or rest in cedar shade.
Are wounded
In yurt or frame or mothers
Shopping at the outskirts in fresh clothes.
Whose sick eye bleeds the land,
Fast it !   thick throat shields from evil,
                    you young girls
First caught with the gut-cramp
Gather punk wood and sour leaf
Keep out of our kitchen.
Your garden plots, your bright fabrics,
Clever ways to carry children
Hide
        a beauty like season or tide,
                    sea cries
Sick women
Dreaming of long-legged dancing in light
No, our Mother Eve: slung on a shoulder
Lugged off to hell.
                    kali/shakti
Where's hell then?
In the moon.
In the change of the moon:
In a bark shack
Crouched from sun, five days,
Blood dripping through crusted thighs.

PIUTE CREEK

One granite ridge
A tree, would be enough
Or even a rock, a small creek,
A bark shred in a pool.
Hill beyond hill, folded and twisted
Tough trees crammed
In thin stone fractures
A huge moon on it all, is too much.
The mind wanders. A million
Summers, night air still and the rocks
Warm.   Sky over endless mountains.
All the junk that goes with being human
Drops away, hard rock wavers
Even the heavy present seems to fail
This bubble of a heart.
Words and books
Like a small creek off a high ledge
Gone in the dry air.

A clear, attentive mind
Has no meaning but that
Which sees is truly seen.
No one loves rock, yet we are here.
Night chills. A flick
In the moonlight
Slips into Juniper shadow:
Back there unseen
Cold proud eyes
Of Cougar or Coyote
Watch me rise and go.

MILTON BY FIRELIGHT
Piute Creek, August 1955

"O hell, what do mine eyes
       with grief behold?"
Working with an old
Singlejack miner, who can sense
The vein and cleavage
In the very guts of rock, can
Blast granite, build
Switchbacks that last for years
Under the beat of snow, thaw, mule-hooves.
What use, Milton, a silly story
Of our lost general parents,
       eaters of fruit?

The Indian, the chainsaw boy,
And a string of six mules
Came riding down to camp
Hungry for tomatoes and green apples.
Sleeping in saddle-blankets
Under a bright night-sky
Han River slantwise by morning.
Jays squall
Coffee boils

In ten thousand years the Sierras
Will be dry and dead, home of the scorpion.
Ice-scratched slabs and bent trees.
No paradise, no fall,
Only the weathering land
The wheeling sky,
Man, with his Satan

Scouring the chaos of the mind.
Oh Hell!

Fire down
Too dark to read, miles from a road
The bell-mare clangs in the meadow
That packed dirt for a fill-in
Scrambling through loose rocks
On an old trail
All of a summer's day.

ABOVE PATE VALLEY

We finished clearing the last
Section of trail by noon,
High on the ridge-side
Two thousand feet above the creek
Reached the pass, went on
Beyond the white pine groves,
Granite shoulders, to a small
Green meadow watered by the snow,
Edged with Aspen—sun
Straight high and blazing
But the air was cool.
Ate a cold fried trout in the
Trembling shadows. I spied
A glitter, and found a flake
Black volcanic glass—obsidian—
By a flower. Hands and knees
Pushing the Bear grass, thousands
Of arrowhead leavings over a
Hundred yards. Not one good
Head, just razor flakes
On a hill snowed all but summer,
A land of fat summer deer,
They came to camp. On their
Own trails. I followed my own
Trail here. Picked up the cold-drill,
Pick, singlejack, and sack
Of dynamite.
Ten thousand years.

WATER

Pressure of sun on the rockslide
Whirled me in a dizzy hop-and-step descent,
Pool of pebbles buzzed in a Juniper shadow,
Tiny tongue of a this-year rattlesnake flicked,
I leaped, laughing for little boulder-color coil—
Pounded by heat raced down the slabs to the creek
Deep tumbling under arching walls and stuck
Whole head and shoulders in the water:
Stretched full on cobble—ears roaring
Eyes open aching from the cold and faced a trout.

FOR A FAR-OUT FRIEND

Because I once beat you up
Drunk, stung with weeks of torment
And saw you no more,
And you had calm talk for me today
   I now suppose
I was less sane than you,
You hung on dago red,
   me hooked on books.
You once ran naked toward me
Knee deep in cold March surf
On a tricky beach between two
   pounding seastacks—
I saw you as a Hindu Deva-girl
Light legs dancing in the waves,
Breasts like dream-breasts
Of sea, and child, and astral
   Venus-spurting milk.
And traded our salt lips.

Visions of your body
Kept me high for weeks, I even had
   a sort of trance for you
A day in a dentist's chair.
I found you again, gone stone,
In Zimmer's book of Indian Art:
Dancing in that life with
Grace and love, with rings
And a little golden belt, just above
    your naked snatch
And I thought—more grace and love

In that wild Deva life where you belong
Than in this dress-and-girdle life
You'll ever give
Or get.

HAY FOR THE HORSES

He had driven half the night
From far down San Joaquin
Through Mariposa, up the
Dangerous mountain roads,
And pulled in at eight a.m.
With his big truckload of hay
      behind the barn.
With winch and ropes and hooks
We stacked the bales up clean
To splintery redwood rafters
High in the dark, flecks of alfalfa
Whirling through shingle-cracks of light,
Itch of haydust in the
      sweaty shirt and shoes.
At lunchtime under Black oak
Out in the hot corral,
—The old mare nosing lunchpails,
Grasshoppers crackling in the weeds—
"I'm sixty-eight" he said,
"I first bucked hay when I was seventeen.
I thought, that day I started,
I sure would hate to do this all my life.
And dammit, that's just what
I've gone and done."

THIN ICE

Walking in February
A warm day after a long freeze
On an old logging road
Below Sumas Mountain
Cut a walking stick of alder,
Looked down through clouds
On wet fields of the Nooksack—
And stepped on the ice
Of a frozen pool across the road.
It creaked
The white air under
Sprang away, long cracks
Shot out in the black,
My cleated mountain boots
Slipped on the hard slick
—like thin ice—the sudden
Feel of an old phrase made real—
Instant of frozen leaf,
Icewater, and staff in hand.
"Like walking on thin ice—"
I yelled back to a friend,
It broke and I dropped
Eight inches in

NOOKSACK VALLEY
February 1956

At the far end of a trip north
In a berry-pickers cabin
At the edge of a wide muddy field
Stretching to the woods and cloudy mountains,
Feeding the stove all afternoon with cedar,
Watching the dark sky darken, a heron flap by,
A huge setter pup nap on the dusty cot.
High rotten stumps in the second-growth woods
Flat scattered farms in the bends of the Nooksack
River. Steelhead run now
                    a week and I go back
Down 99, through towns, to San Francisco
                              and Japan.
All America south and east,
Twenty-five years in it brought to a trip-stop
Mind-point, where I turn
Caught more on this land—rock tree and man,
Awake, than ever before, yet ready to leave.
                    damned memories,
Whole wasted theories, failures and worse success,
Schools, girls, deals, try to get in
To make this poem a froth, a pity,
A dead fiddle for lost good jobs.
                    the cedar walls
Smell of our farm-house, half built in '35.
Clouds sink down the hills
Coffee is hot again. The dog
Turns and turns about, stops and sleeps.

ALL THROUGH THE RAINS

That mare stood in the field—
A big pine tree and a shed,
But she stayed in the open
Ass to the wind, splash wet.
I tried to catch her April
For a bareback ride,
She kicked and bolted
Later grazing fresh shoots
In the shade of the down
Eucalyptus on the hill.

MIGRATION OF BIRDS
April 1956

It started just now with a hummingbird
Hovering over the porch two yards away
                     then gone,
It stopped me studying.
I saw the redwood post
Leaning in clod ground
Tangled in a bush of yellow flowers
Higher than my head, through which we push
Every time we come inside—
The shadow network of the sunshine
Through its vines. White-crowned sparrows
Make tremendous singings in the trees
The rooster down the valley crows and crows.
Jack Kerouac outside, behind my back
Reads the *Diamond Sutra* in the sun.
Yesterday I read *Migration of Birds*;
The Golden Plover and the Arctic Tern.
Today that big abstraction's at our door
For juncoes and the robins all have left,
Broody scrabblers pick up bits of string
And in this hazy day
Of April summer heat
Across the hill the seabirds
Chase Spring north along the coast:
Nesting in Alaska
In six weeks.

TŌJI

Shingon temple, Kyoto

Men asleep in their underwear
Newspapers under their heads
Under the eaves of Tōji,
Kobo Daishi solid iron and ten feet tall
Strides through, a pigeon on his hat.

Peering through chickenwire grates
At dusty gold-leaf statues
A cynical curving round-belly
Cool Bodhisattva—maybe Avalokita—
Bisexual and tried it all, weight on
One leg, haloed in snake-hood gold
Shines through the shadow
An ancient hip smile
Tingling of India and Tibet.

Loose-breasted young mother
With her kids in the shade here
Of old Temple tree,
Nobody bothers you in Tōji;
The streetcar clanks by outside.

HIGASHI HONGWANJI
Shinshu temple

In a quiet dusty corner
      on the north porch
Some farmers eating lunch on the steps.
Up high behind a beam: a small
      carved wood panel
Of leaves, twisting tree trunk,
Ivy, and a sleek fine-haired Doe.
      a six-point Buck in front
Head crooked back, watching her.
The great tile roof sweeps up
& floats a grey shale
Mountain over the town.

KYOTO: MARCH

A few light flakes of snow
Fall in the feeble sun;
Birds sing in the cold,
A warbler by the wall. The plum
Buds tight and chill soon bloom.
The moon begins first
Fourth, a faint slice west
At nightfall. Jupiter half-way
High at the end of night—
Meditation. The dove cry
Twangs like a bow.
At dawn Mt. Hiei dusted white
On top; in the clear air
Folds of all the gullied green
Hills around the town are sharp,
Breath stings. Beneath the roofs
Of frosty houses
Lovers part, from tangle warm
Of gentle bodies under quilt
And crack the icy water to the face
And wake and feed the children
And grandchildren that they love.

A STONE GARDEN

1

Japan a great stone garden in the sea.
Echoes of hoes and weeding,
Centuries of leading hill-creeks down
To ditch and pool in fragile knee-deep fields.
Stone-cutter's chisel and a whanging saw,
Leafy sunshine rustling on a man
Chipping a foot-square rough hinoki beam;
I thought I heard an axe chop in the woods
It broke the dream; and woke up dreaming
                                on a train.
It must have been a thousand years ago
In some old mountain sawmill of Japan.
A horde of excess poets and unwed girls
And I that night prowled Tokyo like a bear
Tracking the human future
Of intelligence and despair.

2

I recollect a girl I thought I knew.
Little black-haired bobcut children
Scatter water on the dusty morning street—
& walked a hundred nights in summer
Seeing in open doors and screens
The thousand postures of all human fond
Touches and gestures, glidings, nude,
The oldest and nakedest women more the sweet,
And saw there first old withered breasts
Without an inward wail of sorrow and dismay

Because impermanence and destructiveness of time
In truth means only, lovely women age—
But with the noble glance of I Am Loved
From children and from crones, time is destroyed.
The cities rise and fall and rise again
From storm and quake and fire and bomb,
The glittering smelly ricefields bloom,
And all that growing up and burning down
Hangs in the void a little knot of sound.

3

Thinking about a poem I'll never write.
With gut on wood and hide, and plucking thumb,
Grope and stutter for the words, invent a tune,
In any tongue, this moment one time true
Be wine or blood or rhythm drives it through—
A leap of words to things and there it stops.
Creating empty caves and tools in shops
And holy domes, and nothing you can name;
The long old chorus blowing underfoot
Makes high wild notes of mountains in the sea.
O Muse, a goddess gone astray
Who warms the cow and makes the wise man sane,
(& even madness gobbles demons down)
Then dance through jewelled trees & lotus crowns
For Narihira's lover, the crying plover,
For babies grown and childhood homes
And moving, moving, on through scenes and towns
Weep for the crowds of men
Like birds gone south forever.
The long-lost hawk of Yakamochi and Thoreau
Flits over yonder hill, the hand is bare,
The noise of living families fills the air.

4

What became of the child we never had—
Delight binds man to birth, to death,
—Let's gather in the home—for soon we part—
(The daughter is in school, the son's at work)
& silver fish-scales coat the hand, the board;
The charcoal glowing underneath the eaves,
Squatting and fanning til the rice is steamed,
All our friends and children come to eat.
This marriage never dies. Delight
Crushes it down and builds it all again
With flesh and wood and stone,
The woman there—she is not old or young.

Allowing such distinctions to the mind:
A formal garden made by fire and time.

Red Sea
December, 1957

THE SAPPA CREEK

Old rusty-belly thing will soon be gone
Scrap and busted while we're still on earth—
But here you cry for care,
We paint your steel shelves red
& store the big brass valves with green
Wheel handles. Dustpan and wastecan
Nestle in the corner—
Contemplating what to throw away.
Rags in bales, the final home for bathrobes,
Little boy bluejeans and housewife dresses
Gay print splash—all wiping oil off floorplates,
Dangling from hip pockets like a scalp.
Chipping paint, packing valves, going nuts,
Eating frozen meat, we wander greasy nurses
Tending sick and nervous old & cranky ship.

AT FIVE A.M. OFF THE NORTH COAST OF SUMATRA

At five a.m. off the north coast of Sumatra

An alarm bell woke me, I slept on a cot on the
                                        boatdeck,
it was deep in the engine-room ringing,
then the lookout's bell on the bow bonged three times
dead-ahead-danger, the engines whined down,
the ship shuddered and twisted,
Full Astern, I jumped up and saw in the dark
dark land: where we never thought island would be.
the ship swung full right and the engines
went dead-slow-ahead
quiet, like drifting.
first dawn in the east making light behind black
                                        island hills,
the morning star broke from the clouds,
and then the breeze came from ashore:
mud leaf decay and soft life of plant jungle:
I went back to the cot and lay breathing it.
after weeks of sea air machine.
the ship found its course and climbed back to full speed
and went on.

GOOFING AGAIN

Goofing again
I shifted weight the wrong way
flipping the plank end-over
dumping me down in the bilge
& splatting a gallon can
of thick sticky dark red
italian deck paint
over the fresh white bulkhead.
such a trifling move
& such spectacular results.
now I have to paint the wall again
& salvage only from it all a poem.

Mind swarming with pictures, cheap magazines, drunk
    brawls, low books and days at sea; hatred of machinery
    and money & whoring my hands and back to move this
    military oil—
I sit on the boat-deck finally alone: borrowing the oiler's
    dirty cot, I see the moon, white wake, black water & a
    few bright stars.
All day I read de Sade—I loathe that man—wonder on his
    challenge, seek sodomy & murder in my heart—& dig
    the universe as playful, cool, and infinitely blank—
De Sade and Reason and the Christian Love.
Inhuman ocean, black horizon, light blue moon-filled sky, the
    moon, a perfect wisdom pearl—old symbols, waves,
    reflections of the moon—those names of goddesses, that
    rabbit on its face, the myths, the tides,
Inhuman Altair—that "inhuman" talk; the eye that sees all
    space is socketed in this one human skull. Transformed.
    The source of the sun's heat is the mind,
I will not cry Inhuman & think that makes us small and nature
    great, we are, enough, and as we are—
Invisible seabirds track us, saviours come and save us.

Recall a cloud of little minnows about our anchored ship in
    the green lagoon of Midway. Corpse of a frigate-bird on
    the beach, a turtle-shell a foot across flesh clinging still—
And out through narrow reefs to sea again, a month to go to
    Persia. All the big wood Buddhas in Japan could bob
    these waves, unnoticed by a bird—
Yesterday was the taste of seawater as I swam; now crack my
    joints, all that I see & miss & never lose floods in—

Damn me a fool last night in port drunk on the floor & damn
this cheap trash we read. Hawaiian workers shared us
beer in the long wood dredgemen's steel-men's girl-less
night drunk and gambling hall, called us strange seamen
blala and clasped our arms & sang real Hawaiian songs,
Bearded and brown and all the blood of Pacific in them
laughing, tattered shirts and tin hats, three-o-five an
hour;
Damn me not I make a better fool. And there is nothing
vaster, more beautiful, remote, unthinking (eternal rose-
red sunrise on the surf—great rectitude of rocks) than
man, inhuman man,
At whom I look for a thousand light years from a seat near
Scorpio, amazed and touched by his concern and pity for
my plight, a simple star,
Then trading shapes again. My wife is gone, my girl is gone,
my books are loaned, my clothes are worn, I gave away
a car; and all that happened years ago. Mind & matter,
love & space are frail as foam on beer. Wallowing on and
on,
Fire spins the driveshaft of this ship, full of smooth oil &
noise—blood of the palms d'antan—sweet oil of the
gritty earth—embraced in welded plates of perfect steel.

CARTAGENA

Rain and thunder beat down and flooded the streets
We danced with Indian girls in a bar,
   water half-way to our knees,
The youngest one slipped down her dress and danced
   bare to the waist,
The big negro deckhand made out with his girl on his lap
   in a chair her dress over her eyes
Coca-cola and rum, and rainwater all over the floor.
In the glittering light I got drunk and reeled through
   the rooms,
And cried, "Cartagena! swamp of unholy loves!"
And wept for the Indian whores who were younger than me,
   and I was eighteen,
And splashed after the crew down the streets wearing
   sandals bought at a stall
And got back to the ship, dawn came,
   we were far out at sea.

Colombia 1948—Arabia 1958

Lay down these words
Before your mind like rocks.
           placed solid, by hands
In choice of place, set
Before the body of the mind
           in space and time:
Solidity of bark, leaf, or wall
           riprap of things:
Cobble of milky way,
           straying planets,
These poems, people,
           lost ponies with
Dragging saddles
           and rocky sure-foot trails.
The worlds like an endless
           four-dimensional
Game of Go.
           ants and pebbles
In the thin loam, each rock a word
           a creek-washed stone
Granite: ingrained
           with torment of fire and weight
Crystal and sediment linked hot
           all change, in thoughts,
As well as things.

COLD
MOUNTAIN
POEMS

HAN-SHAN READING A SCROLL, attributed to Lo-ch'uang
(13th century). Hanging scroll; ink on paper. University
Art Museum, University of California, Berkeley.

PREFACE TO THE POEMS OF HAN-SHAN BY LU CH'IU-YIN, GOVERNOR OF T'AI PREFECTURE

[*Kanzan, or Han-shan, "Cold Mountain" takes his name from where he lived. He is a mountain madman in an old Chinese line of ragged hermits. When he talks about Cold Mountain he means himself, his home, his state of mind. He lived in the T'ang dynasty—traditionally A.D. 627–650, although Hu Shih dates him 700–780. This makes him roughly contemporary with Tu Fu, Li Po, Wang Wei, and Po Chü-i. His poems, of which three hundred survive, are written in T'ang colloquial: rough and fresh. The ideas are Taoist, Buddhist, Zen. He and his sidekick Shih-te (Jittoku in Japanese) became great favorites with Zen painters of later days—the scroll, the broom, the wild hair and laughter. They became Immortals and you sometimes run onto them today in the skidrows, orchards, hobo jungles, and logging camps of America.*]

No one knows just what sort of man Han-shan was. There are old people who knew him: they say he was a poor man, a crazy character. He lived alone seventy li west of the T'ang-hsing district of T'ien-t'ai at a place called Cold Mountain. He often went down to the Kuo-ch'ing Temple. At the temple lived Shih-te, who ran the dining hall. He sometimes saved leftovers for Han-shan, hiding them in a bamboo tube. Han-shan would come and carry it away; walking the long veranda, calling and shouting happily, talking and laughing to himself. Once the monks followed him, caught him, and made fun of him. He stopped, clapped his hands, and laughed greatly—Ha Ha!—for a spell, then left.

He looked like a tramp. His body and face were old and beat. Yet in every word he breathed was a meaning in line with the subtle principles of things, if only you thought of it deeply. Everything he said had a feeling of the Tao in it, profound and arcane secrets. His hat was made of birch bark, his clothes were ragged and worn out, and his shoes were wood. Thus men who have made it hide their tracks: unifying categories and interpenetrating things. On that long veranda calling and singing, in his words of reply Ha Ha!—the three worlds revolve. Sometimes at the villages and farms he laughed and sang with cowherds. Sometimes intractable, sometimes agreeable, his nature was happy of itself. But how could a person without wisdom recognize him?

I once received a position as a petty official at Tan-ch'iu. The day I was to depart, I had a bad headache. I called a doctor, but he couldn't cure me and it turned worse. Then I met a Buddhist Master named Feng-kan, who said he came from the Kuoch'ing Temple of T'ien-t'ai especially to visit me. I asked him to rescue me from my illness. He smiled and said, "The four realms are within the body; sickness comes from illusion. If you want to do away with it, you need pure water." Someone brought water to the Master, who spat it on me. In a moment the disease was rooted out. He then said, "There are miasmas in T'ai prefecture, when you get there take care of yourself." I asked him, "Are there any wise men in your area I could look on as Master?" He replied, "When you see him you don't recognize him, when you recognize him you don't see him. If you want to see him, you can't rely on appearances. Then you can see him. Han-shan is a Manjusri hiding at Kuo-ch'ing. Shih-te is a Samantabhadra. They look like poor fellows and act like madmen. Sometimes they go and sometimes they come. They work in the kitchen of the Kuo-ch'ing dining hall, tending the fire." When he was done talking he left.

I proceeded on my journey to my job at T'ai-chou, not forgetting this affair. I arrived three days later, immediately went to a temple, and questioned an old monk. It seemed the Master had been truthful, so I gave orders to see if T'ang-hsing really contained a Han-shan and Shih-te. The District Magistrate reported to me: "In this district, seventy li west, is a mountain. People used to see a poor man heading from the cliffs to stay awhile at Kuo-ch'ing. At the temple dining hall is a similar man named Shih-te." I made a bow, and went to Kuo-ch'ing. I asked some people around the temple, "There used to be a Master named Feng-kan here. Where is his place? And where can Han-shan and Shih-te be seen?" A monk named Tao-ch'iao spoke up: "Feng-kan the Master lived in back of the library. Nowadays nobody lives there; a tiger often comes and roars. Han-shan and Shih-te are in the kitchen." The monk led me to Feng-kan's yard. Then he opened the gate: all we saw was tiger tracks. I asked the monks Tao-ch'iao and Pao-te, "When Feng-kan was here, what was his job?" The monks said, "He pounded and hulled rice. At night he sang songs to amuse himself." Then we went to the kitchen, before the stoves. Two men were facing the fire, laughing loudly. I made a bow. The two shouted HO! at me. They struck their hands together—Ha Ha!—great laughter. They shouted. Then they said, "Feng-kan—loose-tongued, loose-tongued. You don't recognize Amitabha, why be courteous to us?" The monks gathered round, surprise going through them. "Why has a big official bowed to a pair of clowns?" The two men grabbed hands and ran out of the temple. I cried, "Catch them"—but they quickly ran away. Han-shan returned to Cold Mountain. I asked the monks, "Would those two men be willing to settle down at this temple?" I ordered them to find a house, and to ask Han-shan and Shih-te to return and live at the temple.

I returned to my district and had two sets of clean clothes made, got some incense and such, and sent it to the temple—but the two men didn't return. So I had it carried up to Cold

Mountain. The packer saw Han-shan, who called in a loud voice, "Thief! Thief!" and retreated into a mountain cave. He shouted, "I tell you man, strive hard!"—entered the cave and was gone. The cave closed of itself and they weren't able to follow. Shih-te's tracks disappeared completely.

I ordered Tao-ch'iao and the other monks to find out how they had lived, to hunt up the poems written on bamboo, wood, stones, and cliffs—and also to collect those written on the walls of people's houses. There were more than three hundred. On the wall of the Earth-shrine Shih-te had written some *gatha*. It was all brought together and made into a book.

I hold to the principle of the Buddha-mind. It is fortunate to meet with men of Tao, so I have made this eulogy.

I

The path to Han-shan's place is laughable,
A path, but no sign of cart or horse.
Converging gorges—hard to trace their twists
Jumbled cliffs—unbelievably rugged.
A thousand grasses bend with dew,
A hill of pines hums in the wind.
And now I've lost the shortcut home,
Body asking shadow, how do you keep up?

2

In a tangle of cliffs I chose a place—
Bird-paths, but no trails for men.
What's beyond the yard?
White clouds clinging to vague rocks.
Now I've lived here—how many years—
Again and again, spring and winter pass.
Go tell families with silverware and cars
"What's the use of all that noise and money?"

3

In the mountains it's cold.
Always been cold, not just this year.
Jagged scarps forever snowed in
Woods in the dark ravines spitting mist.
Grass is still sprouting at the end of June,
Leaves begin to fall in early August.
And here am I, high on mountains,
Peering and peering, but I can't even see the sky.

4

I spur my horse through the wrecked town,
The wrecked town sinks my spirit.
High, low, old parapet-walls
Big, small, the aging tombs.
I waggle my shadow, all alone;
Not even the crack of a shrinking coffin is heard.
I pity all these ordinary bones,
In the books of the Immortals they are nameless.

5

I wanted a good place to settle:
Cold Mountain would be safe.
Light wind in a hidden pine—
Listen close—the sound gets better.
Under it a gray-haired man
Mumbles along reading Huang and Lao.
For ten years I haven't gone back home
I've even forgotten the way by which I came.

6

Men ask the way to Cold Mountain
Cold Mountain: there's no through trail.
In summer, ice doesn't melt
The rising sun blurs in swirling fog.
How did I make it?
My heart's not the same as yours.
If your heart was like mine
You'd get it and be right here.

7

I settled at Cold Mountain long ago,
Already it seems like years and years.
Freely drifting, I prowl the woods and streams
And linger watching things themselves.
Men don't get this far into the mountains,
White clouds gather and billow.
Thin grass does for a mattress,
The blue sky makes a good quilt.
Happy with a stone underhead
Let heaven and earth go about their changes.

8

Clambering up the Cold Mountain path,
The Cold Mountain trail goes on and on:
The long gorge choked with scree and boulders,
The wide creek, the mist-blurred grass.
The moss is slippery, though there's been no rain
The pine sings, but there's no wind.
Who can leap the world's ties
And sit with me among the white clouds?

9

Rough and dark—the Cold Mountain trail,
Sharp cobbles—the icy creek bank.
Yammering, chirping—always birds
Bleak, alone, not even a lone hiker.
Whip, whip—the wind slaps my face
Whirled and tumbled—snow piles on my back.
Morning after morning I don't see the sun
Year after year, not a sign of spring.

10

I have lived at Cold Mountain
These thirty long years.
Yesterday I called on friends and family:
More than half had gone to the Yellow Springs.
Slowly consumed, like fire down a candle;
Forever flowing, like a passing river.
Now, morning, I face my lone shadow:
Suddenly my eyes are bleared with tears.

I I

Spring-water in the green creek is clear
Moonlight on Cold Mountain is white
Silent knowledge—the spirit is enlightened of itself
Contemplate the void: this world exceeds stillness.

12

In my first thirty years of life
I roamed hundreds and thousands of miles.
Walked by rivers through deep green grass
Entered cities of boiling red dust.
Tried drugs, but couldn't make Immortal;
Read books and wrote poems on history.
Today I'm back at Cold Mountain:
I'll sleep by the creek and purify my ears.

13

I can't stand these bird-songs
Now I'll go rest in my straw shack.
The cherry flowers out scarlet
The willow shoots up feathery.
Morning sun drives over blue peaks
Bright clouds wash green ponds.
Who knows that I'm out of the dusty world
Climbing the southern slope of Cold Mountain?

14

Cold Mountain has many hidden wonders,
People who climb here are always getting scared.
When the moon shines, water sparkles clear
When wind blows, grass swishes and rattles.
On the bare plum, flowers of snow
On the dead stump, leaves of mist.
At the touch of rain it all turns fresh and live
At the wrong season you can't ford the creeks.

15

There's a naked bug at Cold Mountain
With a white body and a black head.
His hand holds two book-scrolls,
One the Way and one its Power.
His shack's got no pots or oven,
He goes for a walk with his shirt and pants askew.
But he always carries the sword of wisdom:
He means to cut down senseless craving.

16

Cold Mountain is a house
Without beams or walls.
The six doors left and right are open
The hall is blue sky.
The rooms all vacant and vague
The east wall beats on the west wall
At the center nothing.

Borrowers don't bother me
In the cold I build a little fire
When I'm hungry I boil up some greens.
I've got no use for the kulak
With his big barn and pasture—
He just sets up a prison for himself.
Once in he can't get out.
Think it over—
You know it might happen to you.

17

If I hide out at Cold Mountain
Living off mountain plants and berries—
All my lifetime, why worry?
One follows his karma through.
Days and months slip by like water,
Time is like sparks knocked off flint.
Go ahead and let the world change—
I'm happy to sit among these cliffs.

18

Most T'ien-t'ai men
Don't know Han-shan
Don't know his real thought
& call it silly talk.

19

Once at Cold Mountain, troubles cease—
No more tangled, hung-up mind.
I idly scribble poems on the rock cliff,
Taking whatever comes, like a drifting boat.

20

Some critic tried to put me down—
"Your poems lack the Basic Truth of Tao"
And I recall the old-timers
Who were poor and didn't care.
I have to laugh at him,
He misses the point entirely,
Men like that
Ought to stick to making money.

21

I've lived at Cold Mountain—how many autumns.
Alone, I hum a song—utterly without regret.
Hungry, I eat one grain of Immortal-medicine
Mind solid and sharp; leaning on a stone.

22

On top of Cold Mountain the lone round moon
Lights the whole clear cloudless sky.
Honor this priceless natural treasure
Concealed in five shadows, sunk deep in the flesh.

23

My home was at Cold Mountain from the start,
Rambling among the hills, far from trouble.

Gone, and a million things leave no trace
Loosed, and it flows through the galaxies
A fountain of light, into the very mind—
Not a thing, and yet it appears before me:
Now I know the pearl of the Buddha-nature
Know its use: a boundless perfect sphere.

24

When men see Han-shan
They all say he's crazy
And not much to look at
Dressed in rags and hides.
They don't get what I say
& I don't talk their language.
All I can say to those I meet:
"Try and make it to Cold Mountain."

NOTES

The preface:

Feng-kan is reckoned in the traditional line of Zen Masters, but in mid-T'ang the Zen people did not yet constitute a separate Buddhist sect. They were rather a "meditation-group" living in the mountains or the monasteries of the T'ien-t'ai (Japanese Tendai) sect, and the Vinaya (discipline) sect.

Manjusri is the Bodhisattva of wisdom, Samantabhadra the Bodhisattva of love, Amitabha the Bodhisattva of boundless compassion.

A *gatha* is a short Buddhist poem.

A doggerel eulogistic poem, also by Lu Ch'iu-yin, follows the biography: I have not translated it.

The poems:

4—a rare example of a poem in the literary manner. Han-shan usually writes in the colloquial, as very few Chinese poets have done.

5—the gray-haired man is Han-shan himself. Huang is "The Book of the Yellow Emperor" and Lao is Lao-tzu, the *Tao Te Ching.*

15—the Way and its Power, i.e., the *Tao Te Ching.*

22, 23—the full moon, the pearl. Symbols of the Buddha-nature inherent in all beings.

Most of Han-shan's poems are written in the "old-song" (*ku-shih*) style, with five or seven characters to a line.

AFTERWORD

I grew up with the poetry of twentieth-century coolness, its hard edges and resilient elitism. Ezra Pound introduced me to Chinese poetry, and I began to study classical Chinese. When it came to writing out of my own experience, most of modernism didn't fit, except for the steer toward Chinese and Japanese.

Although I had written a fair number of poems, by the time I was twenty-four I was ready to put poetry aside. My thinking had turned toward linguistics, the Whorfian hypothesis, North American oral literatures, and Buddhism. My employment skills were largely outdoors.

So in the summer of 1955 after a year of Oriental languages graduate school, I signed on with the Yosemite National Park as a trail crew laborer. They soon had me working in the upper reaches of the Piute Creek drainage, a land of smooth white granite and gnarly juniper and pine. It all carries the visible memory of the ice age. The bedrock is so brilliant that it shines back at the crystal night stars. In a curious mind of renunciation and long day's hard work with shovel, pick, dynamite, and boulder, my language relaxed into itself. I began to be able to meditate, nights, after work, and I found myself writing some poems that surprised me.

This collection registers those moments. It opens with a group of poems written around the transparency of mountains and work, and finishes with some that were written in Japan and at sea. The title *Riprap* celebrates the work of hands, the placing of rock, and my first glimpse of the image of the whole universe as interconnected, interpenetrating, mutually reflecting, and mutually embracing.

There is no doubt that my readings of Chinese poems, with their monosyllabic step-by-step placement, their crispness—and the clatter of mule hooves—all fed this style. I went from the Sierra Nevada to another semester's study at Berkeley and then a year's Zen study in Kyoto, and nine months in the engine room of a tanker in the Pacific and Persian Gulf.

On my second trip to Japan, with the help of Cid Corman and Lawrence Ferlinghetti, the first edition of *Riprap* (500 copies) was printed in a tiny shop a few streets away from the Daitoku-ji Zen Temple complex. It was folded and bound East Asian style.

The little book moved. After a second Japanese edition of 1,000 was gone, Don Allen's Grey Fox Press picked it up and printed it in America. Don and I decided to add my translations of the T'ang era mountain Chan poet Han-shan. I had started these in a seminar at Berkeley with Chen Shih-hsiang. Chen was a friend and teacher. His knowledge and love of poetry and his taste for life were enormous. He quoted French poetry from memory and wrote virtually any Chinese poem of the T'ang or Sung canon from memory on the blackboard. Chen's translation of Lu Chi's *Wen Fu*, "Prose-poem on Writing," gave me the angle on the "axe handle" proverb "When making an axe handle, the pattern is not far off," as it applies to poetry. (Mind is manifesting mind.)

I would have gone on to do more Chinese poetry translation had I stayed with the academy, but my feet led me toward the zendo.

The idea of a poetry of minimal surface texture, with its complexities hidden at the bottom of the pool, under the bank, a dark old lurking, no fancy flavor, is ancient. It is what is "haunting" in the best of Scottish-English ballads and is at the heart of the Chinese *shi* (lyric) aesthetic. Du Fu said, "The ideas of a poet should be noble and simple." Zen says, "Unformed people delight in the gaudy, and in novelty. Cooked people delight in the ordinary."

There are poets who claim that their poems are made to show the world through the prism of language. Their project is worthy. There is also the work of seeing the world *without* any prism of language, and to bring that seeing *into* language. The latter has been the direction of most Chinese and Japanese poetry.

In some of the riprap poems, then, I did try for surface simplicity set with unsettling depths. It's not the only sort of poem I do. There is a place for passion and gaudiness and promiscuous language. The plain poems that I launched in this book run the risk of invisibility. But the direction they point is perhaps my favorite, and what a marvelous risk!

The poems also made their way back to the Sierra Nevada, where trail crews still place sections of literal riprap. I gather the poems are appreciated as much for their sweat as their art. Veteran trail crew foreman (now historian) Jim Snyder told me how the book is now read by firelight in work camps in the back country.

The collection enters its fourth incarnation in this edition with North Point Press.